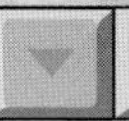

CONTINENTS OF THE WORLD

DISCOVERING NORTH AMERICA'S LAND, PEOPLE, AND WILDLIFE

A MyReportLinks.com Book

Judy Alter

MyReportLinks.com Books
an imprint of
Enslow Publishers, Inc.
Box 398, 40 Industrial Road
Berkeley Heights, NJ 07922
USA

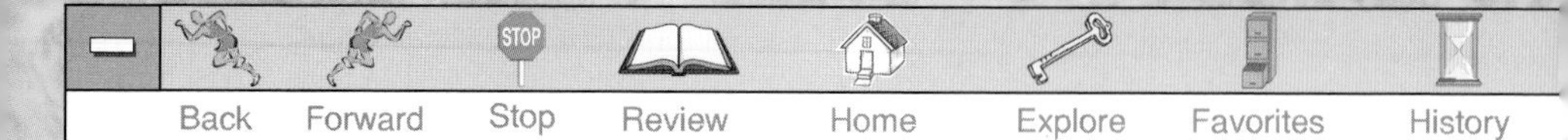

MyReportLinks.com Books, an imprint of Enslow Publishers, Inc. MyReportLinks® is a registered trademark of Enslow Publishers, Inc.

Library of Congress Cataloging-in-Publication Data

Alter, Judy, 1938–
Discovering North America's land, people, and wildlife / Judy Alter.
v. cm. — (Continents of the world)
Includes bibliographical references and index.
Contents: Overview of North America — Land and climate — Plants and animal life — People — Economy — History.
ISBN 0-7660-5206-0
1. North America—Juvenile literature. [1. North America.] I. Title. II. Series.
E38.5.A48 2004
917—dc22
2003014483

Printed in the United States of America

10 9 8 7 6 5 4 3 2 1

To Our Readers:
Through the purchase of this book, you and your library gain access to the Report Links that specifically back up this book.
The Publisher will provide access to the Report Links that back up this book and will keep these Report Links up to date on **www.myreportlinks.com** for three years from the book's first publication date.
We have done our best to make sure all Internet addresses in this book were active and appropriate when we went to press. However, the author and the Publisher have no control over, and assume no liability for, the material available on those Internet sites or on other Web sites they may link to.
The usage of the MyReportLinks.com Books Web site is subject to the terms and conditions stated on the Usage Policy Statement on **www.myreportlinks.com**.
A password may be required to access the Report Links that back up this book. The password is found on the bottom of page 4 of this book.
Any comments or suggestions can be sent by e-mail to comments@myreportlinks.com or to the address on the back cover.

Photo Credits: Artville, p. 1; © 1995–2003 Public Broadcasting Service (PBS), p. 33; © 2001 CanalMuseum.com, p. 16; © 2002 Biology Teaching Organisation/The University of Edinburg, p. 22; © 2002–2003 Family Education Network, Inc., p. 11; © Corel Corporation, pp. 3, 14, 17, 18, 20, 23, 26, 29, 36, 37, 38, 43, 44; © Museum of New France—Canadian Museum of Civilization Corporation, p. 34; Enslow Publishers, Inc., p. 12; Library of Congress, p. 31; MyReportLinks.com Books, p. 4; The Presidency of the Republic of Mexico, p. 40; Wikipedia, p. 41.

Cover Credit: Artville; © Corel Corporation; Photos.com.

Contents

MyReportLinks.com Books

Great Books, Great Links, Great for Research!

The Report Links listed on the following four pages can save you hours of research time by **instantly** bringing you to the best Web sites relating to your report topic.

The pre-evaluated Web sites are your links to source documents, photographs, illustrations, and maps. They also provide links to dozens—even hundreds—of Web sites about your report subject.

MyReportLinks.com Books and the MyReportLinks.com Web site save you time and make report writing easier than ever!

Please see "To Our Readers" on the copyright page for important information about this book, the MyReportLinks.com Web site, and the Report Links that back up this book. Please enter **CNA8913** if asked for a password.

Report Links

The Internet sites described below can be accessed at http://www.myreportlinks.com

*EDITOR'S CHOICE

▶Infoplease Atlas: North America

At this site you can view a map of North America. Click on the different regions to get information about each country.

*EDITOR'S CHOICE

▶InfoUSA

InfoUSA is a United States government site containing facts about American society, politics, and culture. A wealth of resources for studying the United States is provided.

*EDITOR'S CHOICE

▶Government of Canada

The official site of the government of Canada contains information about Canada, including its laws, leadership, and economy. Here you can link to other official sites about the people, environment, history, and geography of Canada.

*EDITOR'S CHOICE

▶Mexico for Kids

Learn about Mexico's history, government, geography, biodiversity, and more. This site also contains news and games.

*EDITOR'S CHOICE

▶1492: An Ongoing Voyage

1492: An Ongoing Voyage, a Library of Congress site, provides information about pre- and post-contact America, the Mediterranean world, Columbus, and European claims in America.

*EDITOR'S CHOICE

▶Emergence of People in North America

It is widely believed that humans first came to North America across the Bering Land Bridge over ten thousand years ago. Read about these first Americans and their journey.

The Internet sites described below can be accessed at http://www.myreportlinks.com

Background Note: Cayman Islands

You can read the United States Department of State's profile of the Cayman Islands. The topics covered include people, history, government, economy, and more.

Background Note: Costa Rica

This is the United States Department of State's profile of Costa Rica. The topics covered include people, history, government, political conditions, economy, and more.

Background Note: Guatemala

The Department of State has an online profile of Guatemala. The topics covered include people, history, government, economy, United States relations, and more.

Belize—A Country Study

This Library of Congress site contains general information on Belize. Find out about the country's history, society, geography, economy, environment, politics, and national security.

Canadian Confederation

The British North American Act of 1867 united Canada's provinces and formally established Canada as a country. Here you will find documents and information related to Canada's slow evolution into a confederation.

canalmuseum.com

The Panama Canal History Museum is an online exhibit about the Western Hemisphere's most well-known man-made waterway. Here you can explore the history of the Panama Canal with photographs, documents, articles, maps, and statistics.

The Deserts of North America

North America contains one of the biggest desert regions in the world. Each of the four major deserts and their wildlife, plant life, rainfall, and climate are discussed.

El Salvador—A Country Study

This site from the Library of Congress Country Studies Area Handbook Program contains information about El Salvador. Topics include the country's history, society, environment, economy, government, and politics.

Report Links

The Internet sites described below can be accessed at http://www.myreportlinks.com

The English on the Chesapeake Bay

Here you can research British settlements in America. Read about the Lost Colony, the settlement at Jamestown, and Maryland's first colony.

The Explorers: Jacques Cartier

In 1534, while searching for the Northwest Passage, French navigator Jacques Cartier came upon the land that is now known as Canada. Learn about Cartier's two Canadian voyages, his routes, and his experiences.

The Explorers: Samuel de Champlain

Samuel de Champlain is known as the Father of New France. Facts about his life, pioneering expeditions, and creation of France's first permanent settlement in Canada are included.

Haiti—A Country Study

This site contains information about Haiti's history, society, environment, economy, government, national security, and more.

Hernán Cortés Arrives in Mexico

This page from PBS provides a brief history of Hernán Cortés's conquest of the land that was to become known as Mexico.

Honduras—A Country Study

This site from the Library of Congress Country Studies Area Handbook Program contains information about Honduras.

Mesoweb—An Exploration of Mesoamerican Cultures

Mesoweb contains a wealth of information about Mexico's indigenous peoples. This is an excellent place to learn about the different cultures as well as hieroglyphic translation, archeology, and anthropology.

Migrations in History: United States–Mexico Borderlands/Frontera

The United States/Mexico Borderlands site from the Smithsonian contains information about illegal immigration, border life, and other issues related to the dividing line between these North American neighbors.

The Internet sites described below can be accessed at http://www.myreportlinks.com

Native North America

This site from Minnesota State University's E Museum contains profiles of dozens of Canadian and United States American Indian tribes. Information about the tribes, their languages, and geography can be accessed.

Nicaragua—A Country Study

Learn about Nicaragua's history, society, economy, government, politics, and more at this site from the Country Studies Area Handbook Program.

Panama—A Country Study

This site from the Library of Congress contains information about Panama. Find out about this country's history, society, environment, economy, government, and more.

PBS—Liberty: The American Revolution

Information about daily life in the colonies during the Revolutionary War. Military perspectives on the war can be found at this site.

PBS: U.S.–Mexican War

The Mexican-American War resulted in Mexico losing almost half of its territory to the United States. In this bilingual PBS Web site, scholars, historians, and authors share their views on the causes, effects, and events of the Mexican-American War.

USTR/World Regions: North American Free Trade Agreement

This site from the office of the United States Trade Representative contains information about the North American Free Trade Agreement (NAFTA). Here you will find a NAFTA overview, the complete text of the document, and a number of other related resources.

Welcome to the Bahamas

Information about the Bahamas is located on this site. History, government, society, economics, national symbols, geography, climate, religion, population, cuisine, art, music, and a number of other topics are covered on this site.

Wikipedia: Mexican Revolution

The Mexican Revolution overthrew the government of Porfirio Diaz and led to the writing of a new constitution. Follow the links in the text of this Web site for a more information on important participants.

North America Facts

Area‡
9,365,290 square miles
(24,256,087 square kilometers)

Population*
480,633,000[1]

Five Most Populous Cities*
- Mexico City, Mexico (8,235,744)
- New York City, United States (8,008,278)
- Los Angeles, United States (3,485,398)
- Chicago, United States (2,896,016)
- Guadalajara, Mexico (2,178,000)

Highest Point of Elevation
Mount McKinley, Alaska (United States) 20,320 feet (6,194 meters)

Lowest Point of Elevation
Death Valley, California (United States) 282 feet below sea level (⁻86 meters)

Major Mountain Ranges
Alaska, Appalachian, Cascade, Coast, Rocky, Sierra Madre, Sierra Nevada

Major Lakes
Athabasca, Erie, Great Bear, Great Salt, Great Slave, Huron, Michigan, Nicaragua, Ontario, Superior, Winnipeg

Major Rivers
Arkansas, Fraser, Colorado, Columbia, Ohio, Mackenzie, Mississippi, Missouri, Nelson, Rio Grande, St. Lawrence, Yukon

Countries
Antigua and Barbuda, Bahamas, Barbados, Belize, Canada, Costa Rica, Cuba, Dominica, Dominican Republic, El Salvador, Grenada, Greenland, Guatemala, Haiti, Honduras, Jamaica, Mexico, Nicaragua, Panama, St. Kitts and Nevis, St. Lucia, St. Vincent and the Grenadines, Trinidad and Tobago, the United States of America

**Population Estimates from 2000 as recorded in Time Almanac 2003.*
‡All metric and Celsius measurements in this book are estimates.

Chapter 1

The Countries of North America

North America is the world's third largest continent. It stretches from the Atlantic to the Pacific oceans. It is almost five thousand miles long from north to south. It reaches from the Arctic Circle to near the equator.[1]

Three countries dominate the continent. They are Mexico, the United States, and Canada. Of these, the United States has the largest population. It is also the wealthiest and most powerful nation in the world. Mexico has about one third the population of the United States. Canada has about one tenth the population of the United States.[2]

The United States has fifty states. Canada has ten provinces and three territories. Mexico has thirty-one states.

Christianity is the most common religion in all three countries. In Mexico, the Catholic Church dominates. Both Catholicism and Protestantism are strong in Canada. In the United States, Protestantism dominates, although there are people from almost every religious groups.

English is the most common language spoken in the United States and Canada. Many people in the United States speak Spanish, as well. In Canada, some people speak only French. More speak both French and English. Spanish is the official language of Mexico. Mexican government officials, educated citizens, and city dwellers often speak fluent English. Most of the poor people in Mexico do not speak or understand English.

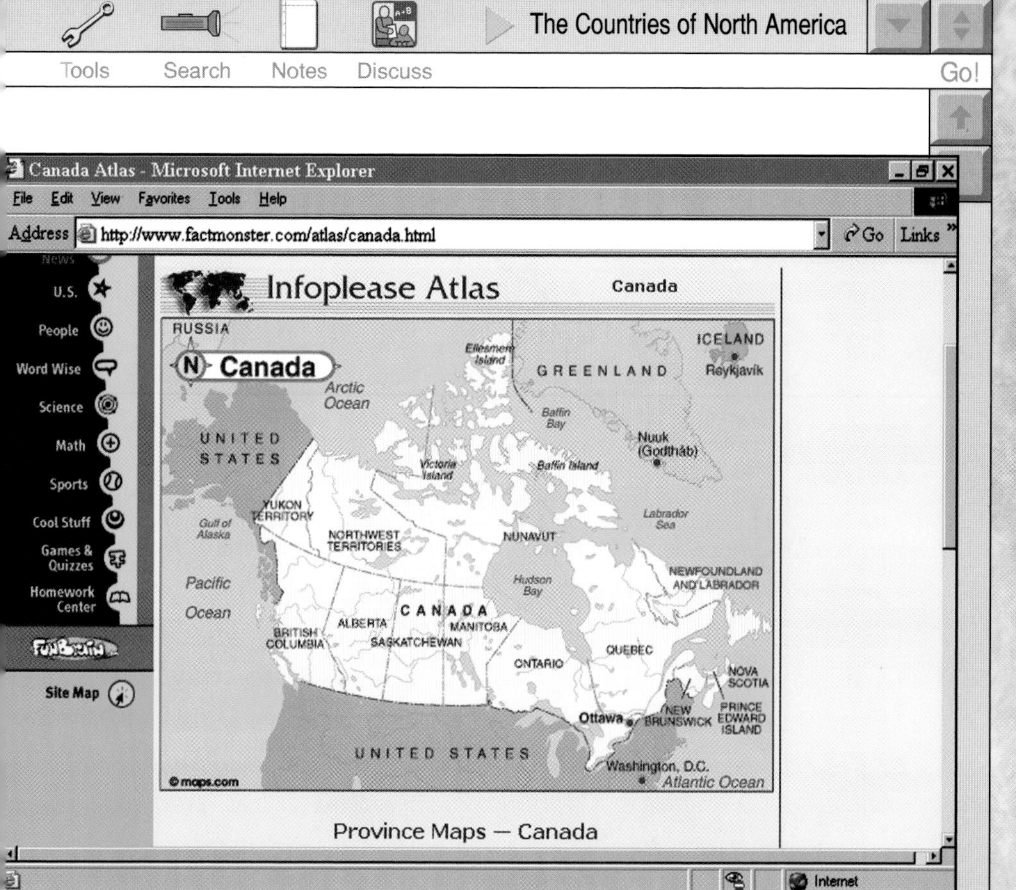

Canada is made up of three territories and ten provinces.

Off the east coast of Canada there lies the world's largest island. This is Greenland. The country has an area of roughly 840,000 square miles. Most of this area is ice.

North America also includes the countries of Central America. They are Guatemala, Belize, El Salvador, Nicaragua, Costa Rica, Panama, and Honduras.

There are also many island nations in the Caribbean Sea that are part of North America. These include Antigua and Barbuda, the Bahamas, Barbados, Cuba, Dominica, the Dominican Republic, Grenada, Haiti, Jamaica, St. Kitts and Nevis, St. Lucia, St. Vincent and the Grenadines, and Trinidad and Tobago. Haiti and the Dominican Republic are part of the same island called Hispaniola.

In addition, there are a number of islands in the Caribbean that were former colonies that have maintained ties to other countries. The United Kingdom (UK) controls Bermuda, the Cayman Islands, Anguilla, Montserrat, and the Turks and Caicos Islands. The UK and the United States have a stake in parts of the Virgin Islands. The United States also maintains partial control of Puerto Rico. Guadeloupe, Martinique, and Saint-Pierre and Miquelon are all under the jurisdiction of France. The Netherlands Antilles is a possession of the Netherlands, and Aruba is a self-governing part of the Netherlands.

A map of North America.

Chapter 2 ▶

Land and Climate

North America's geography differs greatly from place to place. The continent includes the polar lakes and large islands of northern Canada, as well as the tropical regions of Central America and the Caribbean Sea. Yet several countries share geographical similarities.

Mountains

High mountains run parallel to the Pacific Coast from Panama north to Alaska. These include the Rocky Mountains, which cover a good portion of the Western United States. In the United States, highlands such as the Appalachian Mountains run parallel to much of the Atlantic Coast. In Canada, these eastern mountains become the barren cliffs of New Brunswick. In both Canada and the United States, the Great Plains occupy the central land between the mountain ranges. Mount McKinley in Alaska is the highest point on the continent at 20,320 feet above sea level. The lowest depth is in Death Valley (eastern California and southern Nevada), which is 282 feet below sea level.

Mexico, about one fifth the size of the United States, is bordered on the east by the Gulf of Mexico and the Bay of Campeche. This body of water sits between the mainland and the Yucatán peninsula. On the west coast the border is the Pacific Ocean. Oceanfront lowlands lie before high mountain chains on both coasts. The Sierra Madre Occidental mountain range is to the west.

Death Valley, the lowest point in North America, is a deep trench. It is approximately 130 feet (209 kilometers) long and 6 to 14 miles (10 to 23 kilometers) wide.

The Sierra Madre Oriental lies to the east. The Sierra Madre del Sur range is in the south of the country. The highest peak in Mexico, Pico de Orizaba, is 18,410 feet above sea level. These mountains make building roads and railroad tracks difficult.[1]

Rivers

Mexico has few rivers that boats can sail on. Its short rivers run from mountain ranges to the coast. The Rio Grande is an exception. It forms the entire border between Mexico and the state of Texas.

The United States has a connected network of waterways. The Illinois and Ohio rivers flow into the Mississippi River, which leads to the Gulf of Mexico. To the west, the

Missouri River also flows into the Mississippi. In the Southwest United States, the Colorado River has been carving the Grand Canyon for the past 6 million years.

Canada does not have the same network of rivers. Canada boasts the St. Lawrence River, which flows from the Atlantic Ocean to the Great Lakes.

Central America

Central America is a tropical land of dense forests, mountainous terrains, lush lands for grazing, and heavy rainfall. Except for Belize and Costa Rica, Central American countries do not have the beaches that attract tourists. The countries of Central America remain isolated from the world and from each other, partly because they are separated by difficult mountain ranges.[2] The North American continent ends at the Isthmus of Panama. An isthmus is a narrow strip of land surrounded on both sides by water. From 1904 to 1914, the Panama Canal was dredged through this isthmus, connecting the Atlantic and Pacific oceans.

The Caribbean Islands have mostly white sand beaches, deep blue water, and a mild climate. Cuba is the largest island in the Caribbean Sea. Its northern coast is rocky. To the south are marshes, and in the interior are mountains and valleys. Perhaps the most familiar of the other islands are the Caymans, Jamaica, the Bahamas, and Haiti.

Climate

As the geography of the continent varies greatly, so does the climate. Temperatures become warmer the farther south one goes. Winter temperatures are colder in the higher elevations—generally about three degrees for every one thousand feet. In the western cities of Vancouver and Victoria, the climate is milder than in central Canada.

Beginning in 1501 with the Spanish, people attempted to find or create a route connecting the Atlantic and the Pacific oceans through Panama. However, this was not achieved until 1914 with the help of the United States.

Throughout Canada, January is the coldest month and July the warmest.

Similar weather patterns apply in the United States. Temperatures reach the lowest point in January and highest in July or August. In the Southwest, summer temperatures can easily reach 100°F (37.7°C). In the North, winter temperatures can dip well below zero.

In both the United States and Canada, precipitation is heaviest in the east. The American Southwest is a generally dry region where rainfall is often desperately needed. By contrast, the Pacific Northwest—the states of Oregon and Washington and the Canadian province of British Columbia—has heavy rainfall throughout the year. The Northeast—Maine, for instance—has rainfall equal to Seattle, Washington (about thirty-five inches) and snowfall in the same amount. The state of Florida receives well over fifty inches of rain but snow is extremely rare.[3]

In Mexico, the climate is generally pleasant and comfortable. The rainy season is from June to September. The interior sections of the nation and the north tend to see less rainfall. Rain is abundant along the east coast, in the south, and on the Yucatán Peninsula. It is measured in feet, not inches. Winter storms from the north can sweep as far south in Mexico as the beaches at Cancún.

With about 8,235,744 residents, Mexico City is the most heavily populated city in North America.

The Virgin Islands, located in the eastern part of the Caribbean Sea, experience a year-long summer season. Without snow or sleet, perhaps the greatest natural threat to these islands is hurricanes, which tend to strike between June 1 and November 30.

Severe Weather

Severe weather varies with geography. In the North, danger comes from blinding snowstorms and subzero temperatures. In the extreme southern reaches of the continent, flooding and mud slides are problems because of heavy rainfall.

Tornadoes are a danger in the American Southwest, Midwest, and East. Tornadoes are funnel-shaped clouds that dip down from storm clouds to touch the earth. Sometimes they cut a wide path for several miles, destroying everything in their path. Tornadoes are caused by warm, moist air from the Gulf of Mexico meeting cooler air from Canada. The Tri-State Tornado of 1925 was on the ground for 219 miles, causing devastation in Missouri, Illinois, and Indiana. With winds over seventy miles an hour, it killed 695 people.[4]

The Caribbean Islands, the eastern coast of the United States, the states with shores along the Gulf Coast, eastern Mexico, and Central America are all vulnerable to hurricanes. These storms rise out of the Atlantic Ocean and move westward, following unpredictable courses. Some head harmlessly out to sea. Others head for land. In 1998, Hurricane Mitch tore through Honduras and Nicaragua, killing at least eleven thousand people. The storm left several million homeless due to flooding and massive mud slides. The worst natural disaster ever to strike the United States was the Galveston hurricane of 1900. It caused eight thousand deaths and destroyed almost all property on Galveston, an island city off the coast of Texas. Hurricane season is generally from June through October.

Mexico endures volcanic eruptions and earthquakes. In 1985, an earthquake in Mexico City killed thousands.[5] Volcanoes occasionally occur in other parts of the continent, such as the Pacific Northwest.

Plant and Animal Life

Plant life is affected by climate, rainfall, and temperature. North America includes the forests of the Pacific Coast and the grasslands of the Great Plains. It features the bright colors of fall leaves on the east coast, the bare tundra of the Arctic regions in winter. The cactus plants of the desert, and the tropical rain forests of southern regions can be found on the continent as well. Generally, North American vegetation may be divided into tundra plains, coniferous forests, deciduous forests, grasslands, deserts, and tropical regions.

Saguaro cacti are found in the deserts of North America. The Saguaro grows slowly (about one inch per year), but may reach heights of thirty feet.

Tundra and Forests

Tundra is a cold region of large, rocky, treeless plains. This climate is most common in northern Canada and Alaska. Mountain ranges in the United States also have tundra areas. Herbs and shrubs are the principal vegetation.[1]

Evergreen forests grow in Canada, Alaska, major mountain chains, and along the Pacific Coast south to California. Evergreen trees include pine, spruce, and fir.[2] These are also called coniferous forests.

Unlike the trees of evergreen forests, which stay green all year long, the leaves of deciduous trees turn brilliant colors in the fall. The trees are leafless in winter and sprout new growth in the spring. In summer, the forests are dense with growth. Deciduous forests are found mostly in eastern North America.[3] Beech, oak, maple, elm, and hackberry are typical in a deciduous climate. Smaller trees in these forests include flowering dogwood and redbud.

Grasslands, Deserts, and the Tropics

The central part of North America is grassland. The French gave these lands the name "prairie," which means meadow.[4] Sod grasses on these grasslands form dense mats, like a neglected lawn, and spread horizontally. Bunch grasses have tall stems and individual plants do not spread.[5] Human settlement and grazing domestic animals have nearly wiped out the native grasses. In some areas there is a strong effort to restore native grasses to the remaining prairies.

Deserts have high summer temperatures and low rainfall. North America has two major desert regions. One extends from the northwestern United States to Nevada, Utah, and western Mexico. It includes the Great Basin, Mojave, and Sonoran deserts. The Chihuahuan Desert

covers much of southern New Mexico, parts of Texas, and north-central Mexico.[6] Desert plants are generally low shrubs that are widely spaced to take advantage of any ground moisture. Typical plants include cactus, creosote bush, sagebrush, ocotillo, and mesquite.

Tropical vegetation is found in Central America, southern and central Mexico, and the Caribbean Islands. Tropical rain forests are only found in these regions, South America, and some parts of Asia. A rain forest has a dense, low layer of trees, with a few trees that reach higher. These forests also have ferns, Spanish moss, and air plants that grow on the bark of other trees. There are few flowering plants in rain forests. Individual trees drop their leaves at various times throughout the year.

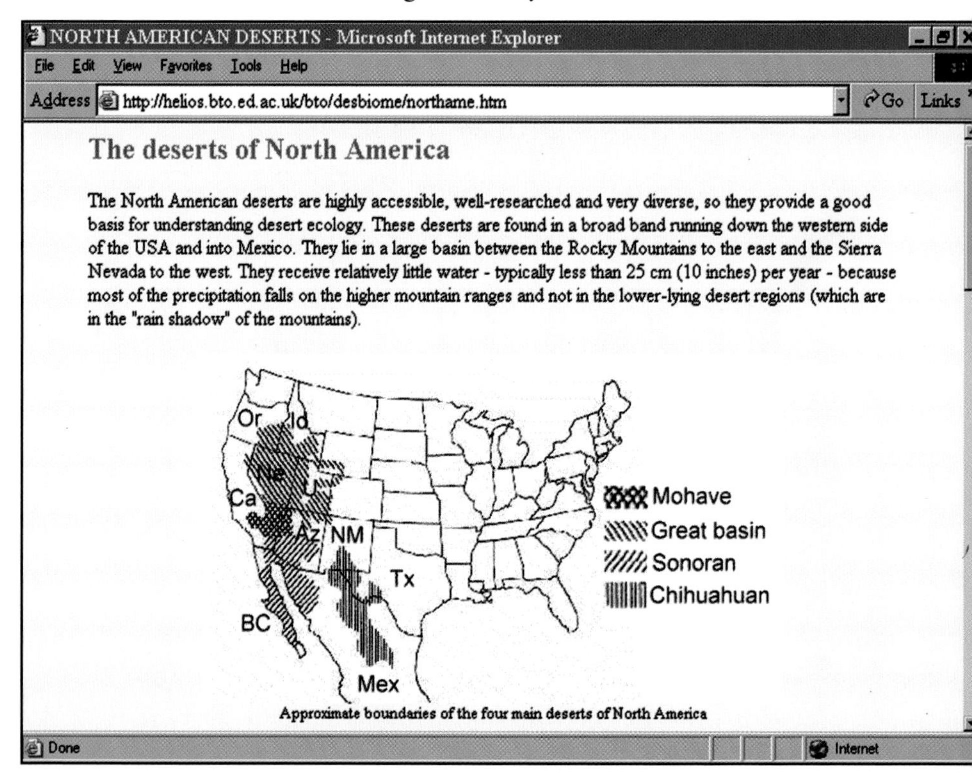

There are four major deserts in North America—the Great Basin, Mojave, Sonoran, and Chihuahuan.

Animals

North America has roughly four hundred species of mammals.[7] Some are found throughout the continent, such as rabbits, beaver, many types of moles and mice, deer, squirrels, some species of turtles, and bats. Whales, seals, and dolphins are found off the coasts of most of the continent.

Animals choose their dwelling by climate. The polar bear, for instance, inhabits a tiny region along the northern tip of the continent. Grizzly and black bears can be found in the United States but are much more common in Canada. So are moose, caribou, and the gray wolf.

Mountain lions, mountain sheep, and the pronghorn tend to be found in the Southwest United States. The opossum, armadillo, and nutria are common in the southeastern part of the country. Elk are found in a small region in the Pacific Northwest.

The tropical parts of the continent have more lizards and snakes. There are three thousand species of lizards in the world. Only a very few are found north of the Mexican border. Most alligators and crocodiles in the world live in the Southeastern United States, especially the Florida Everglades.[8]

Amphibians such as frogs and toads are found throughout North America. The continent also has more kinds of salamanders than all other continents put together.

An abundance of bird species nest in North America. Many of the birds migrate, and fly south to warmer locations in the winter. Some of the birds that can be found on the continent include Canadian geese, ducks, pelicans, and spoonbills. Large amounts of pigeons can be found in the cities of the Northeast United States. One North

The Mexican wolf was once found in the Southwestern United States and throughout Mexico, but the species' range is now limited. Only about two hundred Mexican wolves exist in the world, making it the rarest of gray wolves.

American bird that has been made a comeback toward the end of the 1900s is the bald eagle. It is the national symbol of the United States.

Many species of fish live in the rivers, lakes, streams, and coastal waters of the continent. The oceans provide a great catch of cod, flounder, and shellfish. Crabs are found in the waters of the Pacific Northwest. Lobster populate the waters of the Northeast Atlantic. Fishers in the Gulf of Mexico often catch shrimp.

Chapter 4 ▶

People

The first humans reached North America from Asia well over ten thousand years ago. They are the ancestors of today's American Indians who live throughout the continent. Europeans began to settle what is now the United States, Canada, and Mexico in the sixteenth century.

People From Other Lands

Immigration was a major factor in the development of the United States. Until 1820, immigrants to the United States were primarily from Britain and Germany. In addition, many slaves were taken from Africa and brought to the southern colonies to work the fields during colonial times. Gradually, immigrants came from other countries. These were mostly European countries such as Italy, Ireland, and Austria-Hungary. Many Mexicans and Canadians have also immigrated to the United States. In the late twentieth century, heavier immigration from Asian and Middle Eastern countries increased cultural diversity in the nation.

Canada is a land with two founding cultures—British and French. Today its people remain primarily of British descent with a large French minority. Canada was not open to immigration until after the War of 1812. Then Eastern Europeans settled in Western Canada. These immigrants established farming communes. In recent years, there has been heavy immigration by Sikhs from India, people from Arabic countries, and Jews from European countries.

Mexico had a large native population before the Spanish conquistadors invaded it in the seventeenth century. Today its citizens are mostly of Spanish descent, American Indian, or mestizo—a cross of Spanish and American Indian. Similarly, Central America was inhabited by the Mayans before Spanish conquest of the area. Spaniards killed natives in great numbers. They brought with them diseases such as smallpox, which killed more.

Native Peoples

Of the three major countries, Mexico has the largest native population. In some areas, such as the state of Chiapas, Mayan and Aztec religions continue to exist. Over a million Aztecs still speak the native language, Nahuatl. One of the major challenges to modern Mexico is to bring its American Indian past into the modern economic and social world.[1]

Pueblo Bonito, located in New Mexico, is believed to have been built in stages beginning around A.D. 919. It is an old Navajo dwelling thought to have contained eight hundred rooms at one time.

In the United States and Canada, native populations have also not been treated well. Often the early explorers saw the native population as savages who needed to be converted to Christianity. Expansion of settlement pushed the native peoples westward. Finally in the late nineteenth century, the American Indians were forced to settle on reservations. They had lost their land to Anglo settlement.

Many native people in the United States still live on reservations. They are generally poor and not educated. They have poor health care and living conditions. Alcoholism is a major problem. Reservation American Indians often make their living creating native rugs, pottery, and jewelry to be sold in tourist shops.

In Canada in 1999, the Inuit people successfully created their own government called the Nunavut Territory. This land had been part of the Northwest Territory, a Canadian province. The region had been home to the Inuit for centuries. The citizens of Nunavut make their living fishing, hunting, and trapping. Oil and gas exploration, arts and crafts, and tourism are also large parts of their economy. Nunavut has its own language, Inuktitut.

Both Central America and the Caribbean Islands also have large American Indian populations. Guatemala has primarily a native population. El Salvador, Nicaragua, and Honduras are more mestizo. Panama and Nicaragua have large African-American or West-Indian populations.[2]

Natives dominate the population in most of the Caribbean Islands, too. Their origin, however, can differ according to the settlement of the island. Many islands in the Caribbean have populations descended from Africans imported during the slavery era. Jamaica, for one, has a large population of African descent.

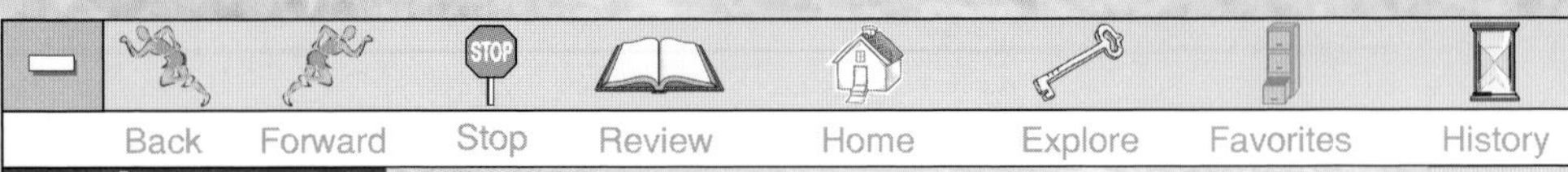

Chapter 5

Economy

The United States is the richest country in North America, and the world. Until the twentieth century, the United States was primarily rural. People lived on farms and ranches and made their living off the land. Today, the agricultural population is small. Most people live in, or near, large cities. The major industries in the United States are construction, service industries (hotels, restaurants, etc.), retail trade, government, manufacturing, finance, insurance and real estate, wholesale trade, transportation, and mining.

Some Wealthy, Some Not

Canada is also one of the world's most successful industrial societies. Canada's primary industries are agriculture, fishing and trapping, forestry and logging, and energy and mining. In 1989, the United States and Canada signed a free trade agreement. Canada relied on the United States for its export trade. Today, its economy is much less wealthy than that of the United States.[1]

Mexico has historically been a poor, rural country. Most Mexicans live in small villages. They raise squash, beans, and corn on patches of land. Many farmers have no modern tools or methods. Mexico's economy is twenty times poorer than that of the United States.[2] There is, however, a smaller privileged, wealthy class in Mexico, primarily in the cities and on the large haciendas (estates).

Mexico's poorer citizens see the United States as a land of plenty where they can escape from poverty. If they cannot enter the United States legally, they sometimes become illegal immigrants. People from Central America also try to cross the border into the United States. Many men from both Mexico and Central America leave families behind, intending to send money to them. In the United States, illegal immigrants are often underpaid and usually live in poor conditions. They oftentimes have little access to health care or opportunity for education. A few Mexicans also periodically go to Canada to find work. Many Mexicans and other Hispanic Americans, however, have entered the United States legally. They have established homes and careers and are important citizens in their communities.

The Caribbean Islands make a lot of money in the tourism industry. T-shirts, hats, bags, and beads are sold on the streets of Jamaica.

NAFTA

In the 1990s, the United States, Canada, and Mexico signed the North American Free Trade Agreement (NAFTA). NAFTA lowered the taxes on the import and export of goods from country to country. A 1999 study showed that there was more trade, business, and jobs in these countries, with Mexico benefiting the most.

NAFTA has softened the borders between the three major countries. NAFTA also made allies of Canada and Mexico and decreased anti-American feelings in those countries. The forging of new relationships between the three countries changed the economic face of the continent.

Central American and Caribbean Economy

Economies in Central American countries remain well below the general North American standard. Most people in those countries live at the level of the poorest of the Mexican population. In the Caribbean, natives often live better because of the high rate of tourism. Outsiders who move to the Caribbean generally only do so because they have the means to live well there, or because they can make more money. For instance, many young Canadian men go to work in the Caymans. The Caymanian dollar is worth a great deal more than the Canadian dollar. After working a few years, these men go back to Canada with accumulated wealth. People from all over the world set up accounts in the Cayman Islands and other Caribbean nations to avoid paying taxes in their homelands.

Chapter 6

History

The North American continent was one of the last land areas in the world to be settled by humans. Between ten thousand and thirty thousand years ago, people migrated to the continent from Asia. It has generally been believed that they crossed on the Bering Land Bridge. This strip of land connected present-day Russia to Alaska. It is now

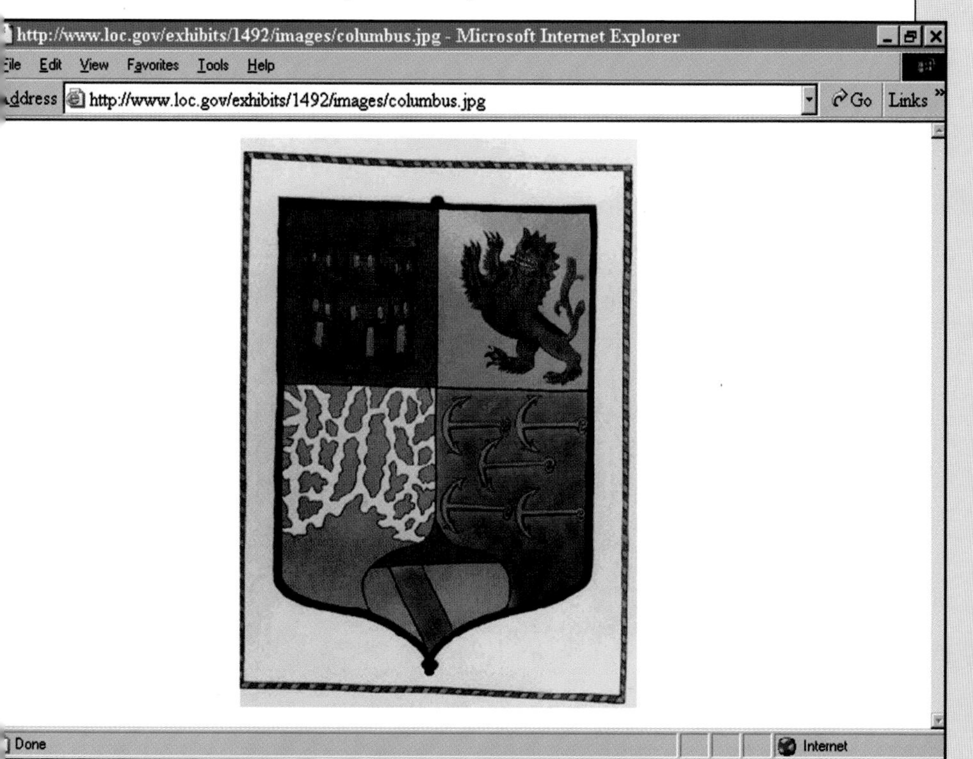

Part of Christopher Columbus's agreement with Spain was that if he was successful in finding a water passage to Asia, he would be granted a coat of arms.

underwater, covered by the Bering Strait. Scientists believe that other people arrived at the same time along the Pacific Coast in seagoing vessels. These were hunting peoples that gradually drifted south. Some went as far as Central America.

European Explorers

When Christopher Columbus sailed from Spain, he did not intend to discover a new land. He was looking for a water passage to Asia. He wanted to buy spices, such as cinnamon. Early explorers, like Columbus, considered the North American continent an obstacle in their way as they searched for a Northwest Passage to the Far East.

However, Christopher Columbus was not the first European to land on the continent. Six hundred years before his arrival, the Vikings had colonies on Greenland. They probably journeyed south to the mainland, but this has not been proven. Later, British sailors came in search of fish, seals, polar bears, whale oil, and walrus tusks.[1]

The North American continent had about 10 million native residents when Christopher Columbus landed in the Caribbean in 1492. These native peoples made use of fire and had some form of religion or belief system. They cared for their land, and many believed they were created from it. Some farmed while others led a nomadic lifestyle of hunting and gathering. Some people lived in the far, frozen north. Others lived in the tropical south. Some were peaceful; some warlike.

The Spanish

Hernán Cortés, a Spanish conquistador, was the first to come deliberately to North America. He came to find gold. Cortés and his men arrived in Mexico with horses in 1519.

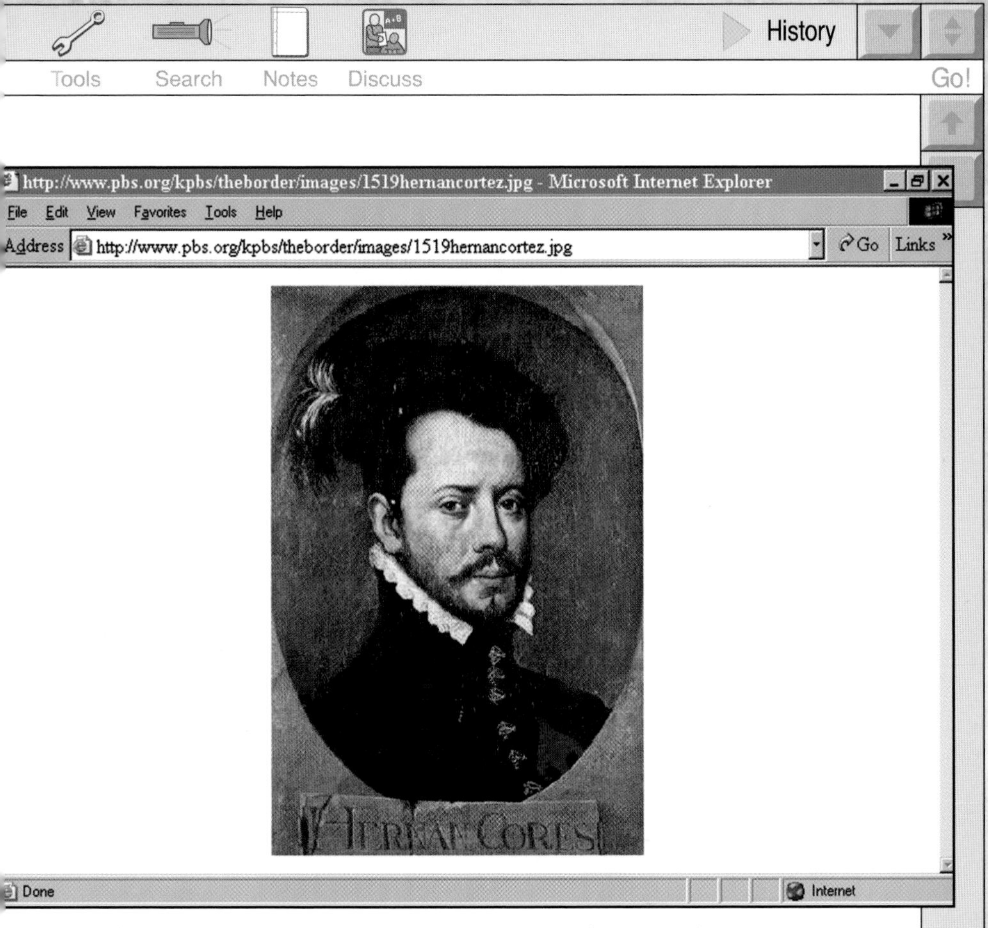

Hernán Cortés arrived in Veracruz, part of present-day Mexico, in 1519. Without permission and against Spanish wishes, Cortés began taking over Aztec territory. By 1521, he and his men had gained control over the entire empire.

The natives had never seen horses, and the strange creatures terrified them. Eventually, Cortés conquered the warlike Aztec people. He stole their wealth and made slaves of them. Cortés built Mexico City on the ruins of their capital of Tenochtitlán.

The French

The French settled unsuccessful colonies in Canada in the early 1500s. In 1534, Jacques Cartier sailed for the North

American continent. He, too, was looking for the Northwest Passage. He did not know that he had discovered Canada. He planted a huge cross on the land in the name of the King of France. Cartier found and named the St. Lawrence River. In 1608, Samuel de Champlain established a permanent colony at Quebec. Champlain is known as the Father of New France.

The British

The British government established its first colony in Canada in 1627. British settlers settled in the central portion of Canada. Quebec remained French in character.

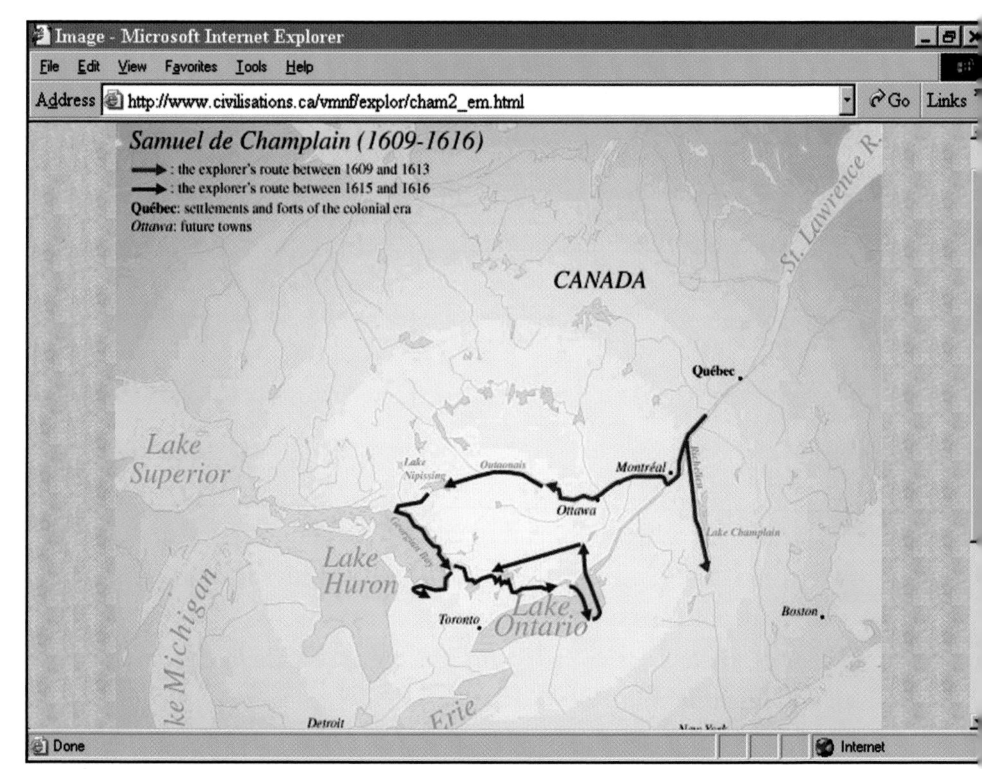

In 1609, Samuel de Champlain returned to the St. Lawrence River to start a fur trade with the American Indians and to look for a passage to China. He continued his search for a route to the Orient on a third trip in 1611.

In May 1607, British ships landed in Virginia and built the Jamestown colony. The Pilgrims arrived in what is now the state of Massachusetts in 1620.

In the late 1600s and early 1700s, France and Great Britain were at war. British settlers on the continent united in an effort to drive the French from the land. After signing the Treaty of Utrecht in 1713, France was no longer a major power, but still owned land on the continent.[2] British colonies in both Canada and the United States grew and prospered. French colonies suffered from neglect. After losing the French and Indian War in 1763, King Louis XV of France ceded control of New France to Britain.

The United States

In the 1770s, Americans refused to follow British laws and pay taxes they thought were unfair. Great Britain sent troops to enforce the laws. Americans fought back in the American Revolution. General George Cornwallis surrendered British troops to General George Washington in October 1781. The 1783 Treaty of Paris formally ended the Revolution. By treaty, the United States acquired huge sections of Canadian land. Lakes and rivers set the country's borders where possible. In 1846, the United States and Great Britain signed the Oregon Treaty. The border between the United States and Canada in the western part of North America would be the 49th parallel. Many Canadians resented the takeover of their land.[3]

Many Americans believed it was their right to control the land from the Atlantic to the Pacific coast. In 1803, France sold its remaining land on the mainland of the continent to the United States. This was called the Louisiana Purchase. It doubled the size of the United States, expanding the nation as far northwest as present-day Idaho.

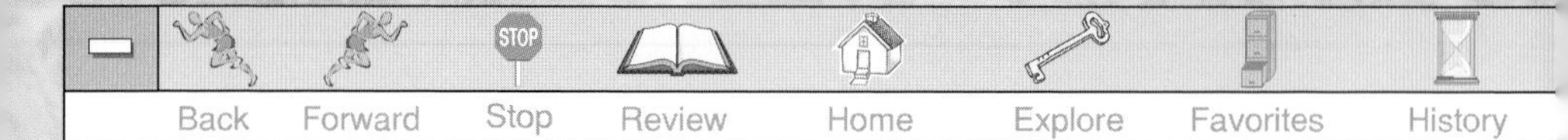

Aside from being one of the most diverse cities in the world, New York City is also a major world leader in finance and communications.

The Spanish Territory, mostly modern-day Mexico, stood in the way of the Americans access to the southern coast.

In the late 1830s, the United States and Canada nearly went to war over the northern border of Maine. The resulting standoff was known as the Aroostook War. The only casualty was one broken arm.[4]

After America's Civil War, from 1861–65 both the United States and Canada had to deal with the native population. America's Indian Wars effectively took all land from the various tribes. Some American Indian peoples, such as Sitting Bull's Sioux, escaped to Canada. On December 15, 1890, Sitting Bull was killed in a gunfight after he had been arrested by the U.S. Army. Eventually all American Indian nations in both countries were confined to reservations. The western frontiers of both Canada and the United States could then be settled by immigrants.

World Wars I and II had a major effect on Canada and the United States. Both joined their European allies Britain and France to fight Germany and Austria-Hungary in World War I, and Germany, Italy, and Japan in World War II. When the Japanese bombed Pearl Harbor in December 1941, Japanese citizens of the United States, Canada, and South America were persecuted. In the United States and in some parts of South America, they were sent to prison camps, called internment camps. These were mostly in the southwestern and western United States. In Canada, they were given a choice of being deported to Japan or staying east of the Rocky Mountains. Some four thousand people were sent back to Japan.[5]

Montreal is the second largest French-speaking city in the world next to Paris, France. Located along the St. Lawrence River, Montreal hosts many festivals in celebration of cultural diversity.

Canada

While the United States flourished, Canada struggled. Britain and the United States fought the War of 1812 over trade issues. Britain had blocked other countries from trading with the United States. The British government soon found the war too expensive. The 1814 Treaty of Ghent reaffirmed America's independence from Britain. The United States got no new territory in Canada but was granted the right to settle Oregon. Canada distrusted the United States, and thought the United States might try to take its land.

Canada at this time was sparsely settled. French citizens greatly outnumbered the British. The country consisted of independent colonies, all governed by Britain. It was not known as Canada. The colonies were referred to individually. In the 1820s, Britain sent many Irish and Scottish immigrants to the provinces. There were continued efforts to suppress the French influence even though the French were the majority.

Ottawa is the capital of Canada. All of its government buildings are located on what is called Parliament Hill.

In 1864, a conference in Quebec chose the name Canada for the united colonies or provinces. The conference established Ottawa, in Ontario, as the new capital.[6] The British North American Act of 1867 formally established the new country.[7] The united colonies remained loyal to Britain. Canada did not seek independence until 1982. At that time, the Canadian Parliament took control of the country, but Queen Elizabeth II remains the head of state.

Mexico

Mexico remained under Spanish rule for three hundred years, from 1521 to 1821. By 1800, the population of Mexico was divided into two distinct groups: the wealthy and the poor. Among the wealthy there was a growing sense of Mexican identity. They were also concerned about poor government by Spain. Spain needed money, and Mexico was its richest colony. Spain increased taxes and made it difficult for sons and daughters to inherit from the wealthy. The 1810 Grito de Dolores (Cry from Dolores) led by Father Miguel Hidalgo Costilla, the parish priest of Dolores, was typical of a series of unsuccessful rebellions.[8]

In 1821, Agustín Iturbide, head of the army, announced a plan that made Mexico independent from Spain. On September 27, he marched his troops into Mexico City. Mexican citizens won independence from Spain. A series of emperors, dictators, presidents, and provisional executives followed. Mexico was weak as an independent country. The country had been ruled by Spain for so long that it had no men trained to lead the government.

Before 1836, Texas was a Mexican state. Most of its residents were Anglos that came from the Eastern

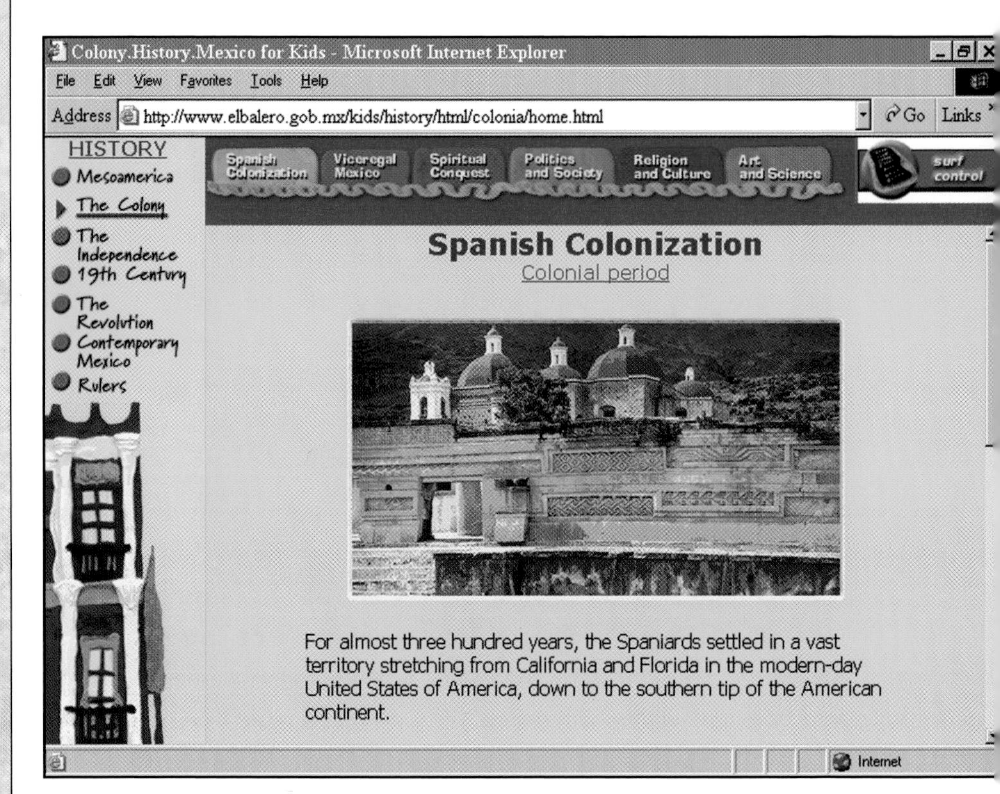

The Spanish had a major impact on the area that is now present-day Mexico by implementing their language, laws, and religion.

United States. They were called Texians. In 1836, they rebelled and fought for independence. The famous battle at the Alamo mission was part of this war. In spite of great odds against them, the Texians won independence. In 1846, Texas became one of the United States.

In 1848, the United States and Mexico went to war. The United States was victorious. The Treaty of Guadalupe Hidalgo ended the Mexican-American War and gave the United States the area that is now much of Arizona, California, Colorado, Nevada, New Mexico, and Utah. The United States then extended from coast to coast. Mexico was humiliated. Like Canada, it distrusted the United States. In 1853, Mexico sold the United States more land in what became known as the Gadsden Purchase. This land is now the southern portion of the states of Arizona and New Mexico.

During the United States Civil War, Napoleon III of France conquered Mexico and installed Maximilian as president. The French initially invaded Mexico with Britain and Spain to force Mexico to pay debt the Mexican government owed those countries. After the United States Civil War, Napoleon withdrew and Maximilian was executed. Mexico was then ruled by another series of presidents and dictators.

From 1855 until 1875, Mexico saw reforms of the power of the church and the military. In 1876, Porfirio

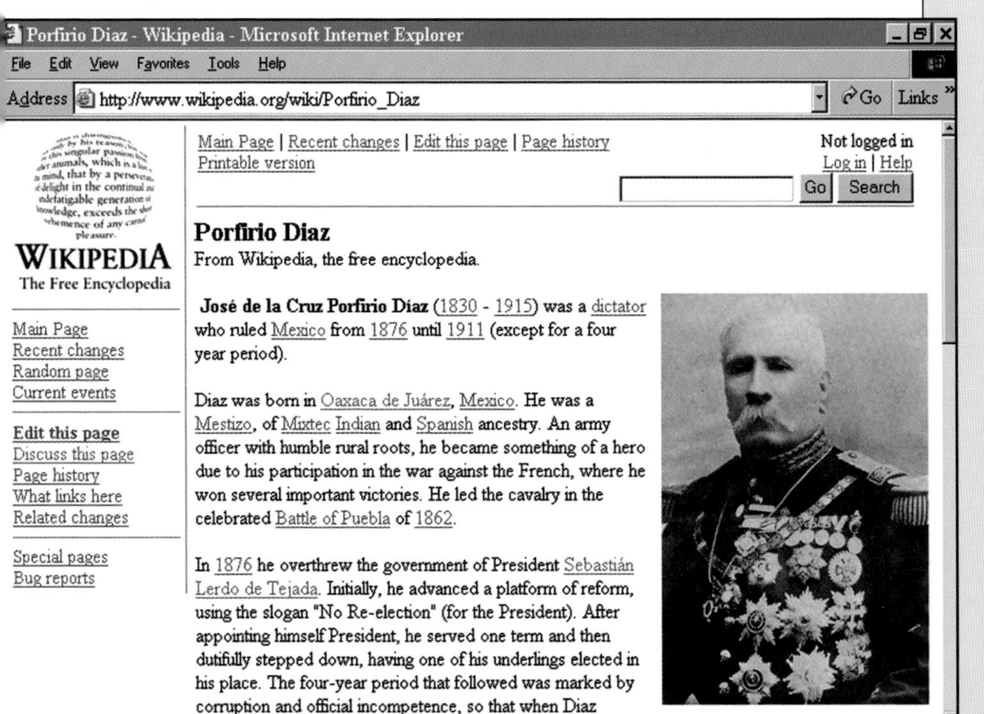

Porfirio Diaz - Wikipedia - Microsoft Internet Explorer

File Edit View Favorites Tools Help

Address http://www.wikipedia.org/wiki/Porfirio_Diaz Go Links

Main Page | Recent changes | Edit this page | Page history
Printable version

Not logged in
Log in | Help

Go Search

WIKIPEDIA
The Free Encyclopedia

Main Page
Recent changes
Random page
Current events

Edit this page
Discuss this page
Page history
What links here
Related changes

Special pages
Bug reports

Porfirio Diaz

From Wikipedia, the free encyclopedia.

José de la Cruz Porfirio Diaz (1830 - 1915) was a dictator who ruled Mexico from 1876 until 1911 (except for a four year period).

Diaz was born in Oaxaca de Juárez, Mexico. He was a Mestizo, of Mixtec Indian and Spanish ancestry. An army officer with humble rural roots, he became something of a hero due to his participation in the war against the French, where he won several important victories. He led the cavalry in the celebrated Battle of Puebla of 1862.

In 1876 he overthrew the government of President Sebastián Lerdo de Tejada. Initially, he advanced a platform of reform, using the slogan "No Re-election" (for the President). After appointing himself President, he served one term and then dutifully stepped down, having one of his underlings elected in his place. The four-year period that followed was marked by corruption and official incompetence, so that when Diaz

Internet

Except for a short four-year period, Porfirio Díaz ruled Mexico with an iron fist from 1876 to 1911. The dictator maintained his power for so long by fixing elections so that he would win.

Díaz acquired power. His government, known as the Porfiriato, reigned until 1910. Porfirio was a dictator, but he brought help to the peasants and American Indians. Investors took an interest in Mexico, and many farmers went to work in factories. Mexico was dependent on foreign business, and the government controlled industries. Revolt against the Porfiriato began in 1910 and was led by men such as Emiliano Zapata and Pancho Villa. Today, they are considered outlaws by much of North America. In 1917, Mexico adopted a new constitution. It is the ruling document of the country today.[9]

The Partido Revolucionario Institucional (PRI) was the governing party of Mexico from 1929 until 2000. During those years, Mexico had great growth in industry and agriculture. During World War II, the country could not import goods, so they began to produce them, which was good for the country's industries. By the 1970s, however, Mexico had to import food. The peso was weak in value compared to the dollar, and Mexico had a huge national debt.[10]

When NAFTA went into effect, people in the state of Chiapas rebelled. Chiapas is a rural state. Its citizens believed NAFTA would benefit only the rich. The revolt revealed corruption in the PRI government.

In 2000, the Partido Acción Nacional rebelled against the PRI and said they would bring honest government, economic progress, and social reform to Mexico. Their candidate, Vincente Fox, was elected president.

The Caribbean Islands and Central America

The Caribbean Islands and Central America are not as involved in international politics or trade as the three major countries. Yet their history is important. Many Caribbean Islands were controlled by Spain after that

country established itself in the New World. In the seventeenth century, Britain captured the islands from Spain. The entire Caribbean was a haven for pirates. The population of many islands was mostly slaves. Slavery was a way for the British to make a profit at a low cost. In the late twentieth century, many islands began to establish their independence. The Cayman Islands, however, chose to stay under British rule.

In Central America, the nineteenth century saw a wide variety of dictatorships in the various countries. There was unity between them to fight common enemies at times. In 1823, American President James Monroe issued the Monroe Doctrine. In it he called for European nations to leave Hispanic-American countries alone and for an end to colonization. In the twentieth century, the United States developed railroads and shipping in the region because it wanted the fruit trade. The principal

Christopher Columbus landed on the Cayman Islands on May 10, 1503, during his fourth and final voyage to the New World. He named them Las Tortugas, or The Turtles, for the large numbers of turtles found on two of the three islands.

Guatemala is located in Central America just below Mexico. It is just one of the many countries located on this part of the continent that have been plagued by poverty. About 75 percent of its population lives below the poverty line.

crops of Central America are coffee and bananas. In the latter half of the twentieth century, Central America was characterized by political instability and poverty. It was also the source of many drugs coming to the United States. When NAFTA went into effect, Central America was excluded.

Working Together

The United States, Canada, and Mexico continue to dominate the North American continent. In 2000 and 2001, all three countries elected new leaders—Jean Chrétien in Canada, Vicente Fox in Mexico, and George W. Bush in the United States. These leaders recognized the importance of a strong North American identity. In many ways, the borders between the countries have shrunk.

Chapter Notes

North America Facts

1. Population estimates from *Time Almanac 2003,* Borgna Bruner, ed., (Boston: Information Please, 2002).

Chapter 1. The Countries of North America

1. Anthony DePalma, *Here: A Biography of the New American Continent* (New York: Public Affairs, 2001), p. 148.

2. *Student Handbook* (Nashville, Tenn.: The Southwestern Company, 1991), p. 164.

Chapter 2. Land and Climate

1. Burton Kirkwood, *The History of Mexico* (Westport, Conn.: Greenwood Press, 2000), p. 3.

2. Lawrence A. Herzog, ed., *Changing Boundaries in the Americas: New Perspectives on the U.S.-Mexican, Central American, and South American Borders* (San Diego: University of California at San Diego, 1992), p. 13.

3. Rick Cech, "Florida Subtropical Forests," Bird Habitats, n.d., <http://www.enature.com/habitats/show_sublifezone.asp?sublifezoneID=18> (October 20, 2003).

4. Ibid.

5. Kirkwood, p. 3.

Chapter 3. Plant and Animal Life

1. John L. Vankat, *The Natural Vegetation of North America* (New York: John Wiley & Sons, 1979), p. 71.

2. Ibid., p. 96.

3. Ibid., p. 132.

4. Ibid., p. 158.

5. Ibid., p. 165.

6. Ibid., p. 180.

7. *North American Wildlife: Mammals, Reptiles, and Amphibians* (Pleasantville N.Y.: Reader's Digest Association, 1998), p. 8.

8. Ibid., p. 92.

Chapter 4. People

1. Anthony DePalma, *Here: A Biography of the New American Continent* (New York: Public Affairs, 2001), pp. 253–254.

2. Lawrence A. Herzog, ed., *Changing Boundaries in the Americas: New Perspectives on the U.S.-Mexican, Central American, and South American Borders* (San Diego: University of California at San Diego, 1992), p. 13.

Chapter 5. Economy

1. Anthony DePalma, *Here: A Biography of the New American Continent* (New York: Public Affairs, 2001), p. 92.

2. Ibid.

Chapter 6. History

1. June Callwood, *Portrait of Canada* (New York: Doubleday & Company, 1981), p. 1.

2. Ibid., p. 24.

3. Anthony DePalma, *Here: A Biography of the New American Continent* (New York: Public Affairs, 2001), p. 8.

4. Callwood, pp. 138–139.

5. Ibid., p. 292.

6. Ibid., p. 166.

7. Ibid., p. 300; DePalma, p. 84.

8. Burton Kirkwood, *The History of Mexico* (Westport, Conn.: Greenwood Press, 2000), pp. 81–82.

9. Ibid., p. 155.

10. Ibid., p. 191.

Further Reading

Bianchi, John-Paul. *North America.* Farmington Hills, Mich.: Blackbirch Press, Incorporated, 2001.

Bouchard, David and Henry Ripplinger. *If You're Not from the Prairie.* Custer, Wash.: Orca Books, n.d.

Cameron, Sarah. *Footprint Caribbean Islands Handbook 2002: The Travel Guide.* Bath, United Kingdom: Footprint Handbooks, 2002.

Green, David. *DK Geography of the World.* New York: DK Publishing, 1996.

Hacker, Carlotta. *The Kids Book of Canadian History.* Niagara Falls, N.Y.: Kids Can Press, 2002.

Hakim, Joy. *A History of the US.* New York: Oxford University Press, 2002.

Kalman, Barbara. *Canada: The Land.* New York: Crabtree Publishing, 2001.

______. *Mexico: The Culture.* New York: Crabtree Publishing, 2001.

Kochanoff, Peggy. *A Field Guide to Nearby Nature—Fields and Woods of the Midwest and East Coast.* Missoula, Mont.: Mountain Press, 1994.

Kozleski, Lisa. *The Leeward Islands.* Broomall, Pa.: Mason Crest, 2003.

Orr, Tamra. *The Windward Islands.* Broomall, Pa.: Mason Crest, 2003.

Peterson, Roger Tory. *A Field Guide to the Birds of Eastern and Central North America.* New York: Houghton Mifflin, 2002.

Sandak, Cass R. *North America.* Austin, Tex.: Raintree Steck-Vaughn Publishers, 1998.

Zinn, Howard. *A People's History of the United States: 1492 to the Present.* New York: Harper Perennial, 2001.

Back
Forward
STOP
Stop
Review
Home
Explore
Favorites
History

Index